1

Mr. Humphrey's Book of Math Poetry
Copyright © 2017
Michael J Humphrey

IF YOU WANT GOOD GRADES, THIS IS WHAT YOU DO
FIND A GOOD FRIEND WHO WANTS THEM TOO

WHEN YOU GET TOGETHER, YOU CAN STUDY
IT'S ALWAYS EASIER WITH A BUDDY

I MADE SOME POETRY FOR YOU BELOW
TO HELP YOU THROUGH
WHEN IT GETS SLOW

Introduction

Hi, I'm Mr. Humphrey, a math teacher in Saint Paul, Minnesota. I've been teaching math for over 23 years, and every year I try new and diverse ways of introducing math to my students. Last year, I tried writing poetry based on each one of the lessons that I taught. Each poem highlights main points in the lesson.

I would like to dedicate this book to my grandchildren: James Junior, Jazmin, and Pennylue. And, of course, to all my wonderful students who truly inspired me.

Contents

Angles and Lines

Once again we hear from the source
Geometry is full of vocab, of course

In today's lesson you'll do just fine
We get to learn about angles and lines

The first pair of lines are called parallel
They don't intersect, but that's not all

If they're not coplanar, don't you see?
They won't be parallel to you or me

If they don't intersect, and aren't coplanar
We call them skew, nothing saner

Perpendicular lines another story
They're always right, and get all the glory

Transversals cut right through
Two or more points of lines so true

Pairs of angles are formed in kind
Transversals cutting through parallel lines

Corresponding angles are just what I said
Same relative position to each other we read

Interior angles are between the lines,
The exterior ones are outside that's fine

Alternate interior angles are on opposite sides of the transversal
They are not adjacent, truly universal

Same side interior are between the lines too
But they don't alternate like the other ones do

Just a thing or two about angles and lines
You need to know these if you want to do fine

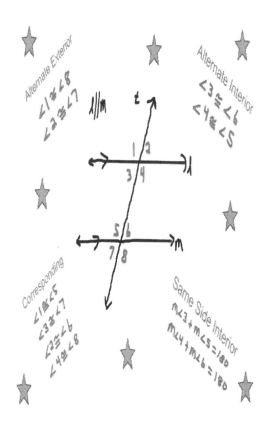

Transversal Two Parallel Lines

When transversals cross through parallel lines
Something happens truly divine

Alternate interior are congruent
Same for corresponding, they have affluence

Not so true for same side interior
They're supplementary, helping the needier

These are some facts that you need to know
Daily practice keeps you on the go

Perpendicular Lines

Perpendicular lines are real divine
Always right, all the time

Intersecting at ninety degrees
Perpendicular lines form like a breeze

Now if crossing lines form linear pairs of two congruent angles
These lines are perpendicular, no need to fret or wrangle

If a transversal is perpendicular to one of two parallel lines
It's perpendicular to the other one, all the time

If two coplanar lines are perpendicular to another
These lines are definitely parallel to each other

Another little tidbit, always true
Shortest distance from a line to a point is perpendicular too

So listen very carefully to the lesson that I give
Brought by your humble teacher, a reason I live

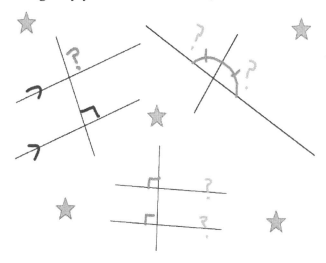

Point Line Plane

Point, line, plane are terms undefined
Thus we give their details, from this we do just fine

A plane is clever —its length and width go on forever.
Just a flat surface, there's no need to sweat or weather

A line comes along with no beginning or no end
It has no width, so we can call it our best friend

A point is a tiny dot, so infinitely small,
 It gives up the location, nothing more at all

You need to know them, it's just a part of school
Getting good grades is what really makes you cool

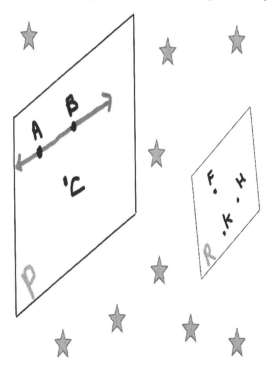

Point Line Plane 2

We designate a point with a capital letter
When we place the dot, it even gets better

Any two points can designate a line
As long as they're on it at the drop of a dime

If we have three points that don't line up
We designate a plane, that's what's up

Giving two letters without a proper symbol?
 You really can't tell if it's a line, or something simple

If you want collinear, this is what you do
Make sure the points line up, then it comes true

For coplanar, let's make a purchase
Make sure the points are on the same surface

Just a quick summary of a couple things or two
Because your teacher cares about you

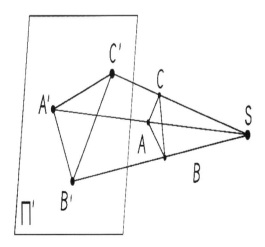

The Algebra of Points, Lines and Planes

To plot a coordinate point, you need an ordered pair
The X before the Y, in the alphabet it's there

To make a straight line, this is what you do
Plot two points, and draw straight through

Making line segments is just as easy
Just connect the dots, nothing cheesy

To find the middle point this is what you do
Add them all up and divide by two

If you want to find the distance, that's okay
Mr. H is going to show the way

Just subtract the Xs, and the Y values too
Square them all up and add them through

When you get done, just take the square root
You have the distance, let's plan the route

Finding the slope is just as fun
Just take the rise and divide by the run

Another way to do it is just as cool
Use the slope formula taught in school

In the numerator subtract the y's
The same in the denominator the x's fly

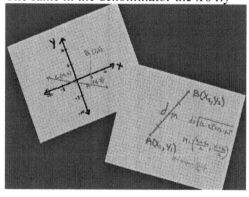

Angles

Today is a great day, can't you see?
We get to learn our angles fundamentally

Take two rays, and connect the endpoints,
You have an angle, and that's the main point

If the rays open up at 90 degrees
You have the right angle for planting trees

The next kind of angle is so cuddly and cute
It's less than 90, so we call it Acute

If it's more than 90, we have nothing to lose
And if it's not quite straight, we can call it Obtuse

Really don't want to be a bore,
But I have to add just one more.

If the angle stretches out to a line
Just call it a straight angle, that is fine

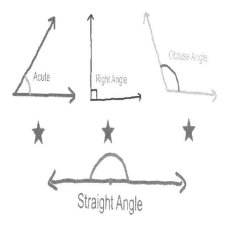

Pairs of Angles

A thing about geometry
You must know your vocabulary

Today we'll study pairs of angles
Yes that's two, I didn't dangle

The first pair of angles I can see
Is adjacent to you and me

They share a vertex and a side
No points in common, on the inside

For another pair of angles just cross two lines
Vertical Angles are formed in kind

Vertical Angles are across from each other
They are not adjacent, that's another

A favorite pair for Mr. Humphrey
Are angles that are complementary

If the sum of their measures turns out right
They complement each other, that is tight

The next pair sounds like dinner, see
We call them supplementary

We put them together, it sure is great
Their measures add up to something straight

The last pair of angles is really fine
They stand together on a line

So please don't stare, you must beware
We call these angles linear pairs

Not only are they adjacent to
But supplementary all the way through

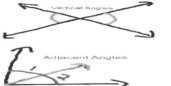
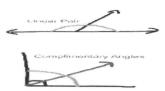

Inductive and Deductive Reasoning

Conjecture is a fancy word
An educated guess, so I've heard

A conjecture based on previous patterns
You've reasoned inductively, turned on the lantern

One word of caution before we get through
Your conjecture doesn't always come true

Any outcome showing the conjecture fails
Is false by counterexample, please don't wail

Now if you want to prove your conjecture true
Deductive reasoning is there for you

You argue based on facts and logic
Your case is proved, you cannot stop it

Whoever thought geometric knowledge
Would develop skills to get into college?

Conditional Statements

Any statement using if-then form
A conditional statement will conform

If hypothesis, then conclusion
Let us avoid any confusion

When you interchange the hypothesis and conclusion
You have the converse, not an illusion

When you negate the conditional too
We call it the inverse, that's what we do

Now contrapositive is just a word
It's the converse of the inverse, that's what I've heard

Deductive Reasoning

Verifying that your conjecture is true
Deductive reasoning will get you through

Conclusions based on facts and logic
You'll prove your case, no need to dodge it

Law of detachment, the conditional true
P is true, then so is Q

The law of syllogism, it's what I say
It's a chain reaction all the way

If P then Q and Q then R,
P then R will get you far

Have a good day I hope you do
I know this poem will help you through

	Deductive Reasoning	Inductive Reasoning
Premises	Stated as facts or general principles ("It is warm in the summer in Spain.").	Based on observations of specific cases ("All crows Knut and his wife have seen are black.").
Conclusion	Conclusion is more special than the information the premises provide. It is reached directly by applying logical rules to the premises.	Conclusion is more general than the information the premises provide. It is reached by generalizing the premises' information.
Validity	If the premises are true, the conclusion must be true.	If the premises are true, the conclusion is probably true.
Usage	More difficult to use (mainly in logical problems). One needs facts which are definitely true.	Used often in everyday life (fast and easy). Evidence is used instead of proved facts.

Algebraic Proof

If you want to win the case, this is what you do
Learn to argue logically, all the way through

Algebraic proof is just one of the ways
You can present your case and win today

An argument based off algebraic rules
It's a logical flow, and helps you through school

The flow of steps that leads to a conclusion
You prove your case, and avoid the confusion

So listen to the rules presented to you
I know you can do it, I will help through

Prove that the sum of two odd integers is even.

Let k represent any integer value, then 2k is even since
even numbers are multiples of 2. Now if you add 1 to
any even, you get an odd. Therefore, 2k + 1 is odd.

By similar reasoning, 2m + 1 is odd.

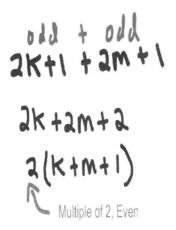

$$\underset{\text{odd}}{2k+1} + \underset{\text{odd}}{2m+1}$$

$$2k + 2m + 2$$

$$2(k+m+1)$$

Multiple of 2, Even

Classifying Triangles

It has three sides, with three angles
Many different shapes are called triangles

To name a triangle by certain characteristics
We call that classifying, nothing futuristic

A type of classifying we can treasure
Goes according to the angle's measure

An acute triangle look and see
All its angles are less than ninety

Equiangular is what some are called
Three congruent angles, that says it all

Another triangle that's trouble for me
It's called obtuse, one angle agrees

And then there's one that's always right
Its ninety-degree angle always in sight

Time to switch to a brand-new station
Looking to the sides for classification

When all three sides are surely congruent
It's called equilateral amongst the affluent

When only two sides come to agree
Call it isosceles, you'll be set free

When all the sides are different too
It's called scalene and now we're through

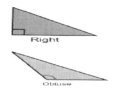
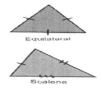

Angle Relationships in Triangles

Today we work to improve relations
Angles in triangles are the big sensation

Sum the three angles of the interior
It's always 180, it can't be clearer

You know two angles? This is what to do
Subtract from 180, get the third one too

Equiangular triangle, angles are the same
Each must be 60, no playing games

Another cool feature, don't feel blue
We have exterior angles, each vertex there are two

They form a linear pair, with each interior angle
Sum of the Remote ones, for every kind of triangle

So please listen carefully, to the lesson through
I have some more vocabulary, especially for you

CPCTC

Two congruent triangles, with corresponding parts
All of them congruent, knew it from the start

CPCTC, from this we all agree
Corresponding parts congruent, in triangles just for thee

It's used in various proofs, throughout geometry
We get to learn the theorems, knowledge sets you free

So pay careful attention to what I have to say
CPCTC will make you feel okay

Triangle Congruence

If you want to be of great influence
You need to learn triangle congruence

If the three sides are congruent to the other
Side-Side-Side (SSS) for my sister and my brother

Side-Angle-Side (SAS) is another one to use
To show two triangles, congruent just for you

Another kind of congruence we shouldn't leave out
Angle-Side-Angle (ASA), sing it with a shout

Angle-Angle-Side (AAS) makes me want to glide
Triangles are congruent, no need to even try

If the letters spell an inappropriate word (AS?)
There is no congruence, that is what I've heard

By this time next week is through
I hope this poem makes more sense to you

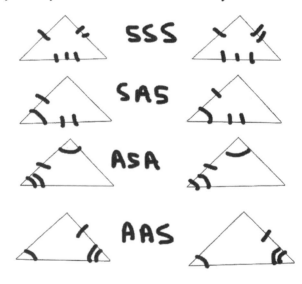

Isosceles and Equilateral Triangle's

It is time to see from another angle
The study of Isosceles and Equilateral triangles

Triangles appear in nature and art
Angles, and sides, and congruent parts

Angles across from congruent sides congruent
Converse also true for the student

If it's equilateral we all agree
Also equiangular, yes all three

So study really hard, it'll be a breeze
Learning about equilateral and isosceles

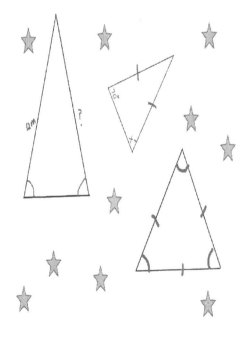

Plotting Ordered Pairs

Plotting points using Cartesian Coordinates
The x-y system in case you didn't know it

Horizontal and vertical distance from origin
Location given of the point forbidden

Take X before Y to find your location
Horizontal then vertical from the origins station

Finish your homework before class is through
Then study vocabulary like we always do

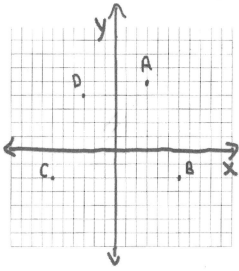

A(3, 5)

B(6, -2)

C(-6, -2)

D(-3, 4)

A point is a tiny dot so infinitely small. It gives up the location, nothing more at all.

Simplifying Radicals

One thing not to tolerate, we'll talk about this later
When my geo-students, show radical behavior

A type of radical, I like much better
Is a square and rootish type, to the letter

Simplifying square roots? This is one is for you
Learn the perfect squares, it's really nothing new

Factoring square roots with perfect square factors
You'll simplify them out, no need to be an actor

Square root all the perfect factors found
Multiply together and simplify sound

When you get done put it together
You simplified a radical exactly to the letter

$$2^2 = 4$$
$$3^2 = 9$$
$$4^2 = 16$$
$$5^2 = 25$$
$$6^2 = 36$$
$$7^2 = 49$$
$$\vdots$$

$$\sqrt{50} = \sqrt{25}\,\sqrt{2}$$
$$= 5\sqrt{2}$$

$$\sqrt{108} = \sqrt{36}\,\sqrt{3}$$
$$= 6\sqrt{3}$$

Sum of Interior Angles of a Polygon

Angles of a triangle sum to 180
According to the sides, and not Tom Brady

For other polygons, this is what you do
Count the number of sides, and then subtract 2

You get the number of triangles, existing in the shape
Each is 180, An angle sum so great

A very nice formula, just like gravy
Just take n-2 and multiply by 180

$$\text{Angle Sum} = (n-2)180$$

Name of Shape	# Sides	Angle Sum
Triangle	3	$(3-2)(180) = 180°$
Quadrilateral	4	$(4-2)(180) = 360°$
Pentagon	5	$(5-2)(180) = 540°$
Hexagon	6	$(6-2)(180) = 720°$
Heptagon	7	$(7-2)(180) = 900°$

$$m\angle 1 + m\angle 2 + m\angle 3 + m\angle 4 + m\angle 5 + m\angle 6 + m\angle 7 = 900°$$

26

Exterior Angles Theorem

Sum the exterior angles, one at each vertex
You get 360, appearing on the surface

It doesn't really matter, 50 sides or 3
360 for exterior angles, please

Another fact you should beware
Interior and exterior form linear pairs

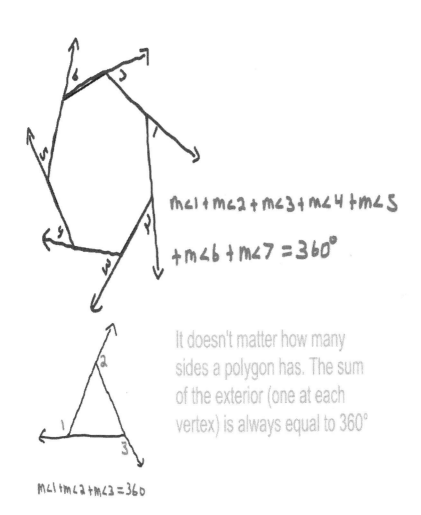

$$m\angle 1 + m\angle 2 + m\angle 3 + m\angle 4 + m\angle 5$$
$$+ m\angle 6 + m\angle 7 = 360°$$

It doesn't matter how many
sides a polygon has. The sum
of the exterior (one at each
vertex) is always equal to 360°

$$m\angle 1 + m\angle 2 + m\angle 3 = 360$$

Similar Polygons

Similar polygons have the same shapes
Though many different sizes, their uses are great

Their corresponding sides are proportional
It's angles congruent, and that's not all

To indirectly measure a variety of lengths
Proportionality is the number one strength

Set up proportions with unknown sides
Next we find them, they cannot hide

Triangle Angle Bisector Theorem

Angle bisector, divides the side opposite
Proportional to the others, to stay on top of it

Set up a proportion, find unknown parts
The bisector theorem, a good place to start

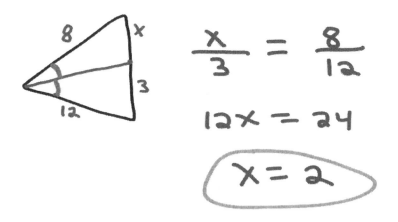

Ratio & Proportion

Today we learn about ratio and proportion
No funny faces or looks of contortion

A ratio of two numbers a over b
Just make a fraction to set you free

When two ratios equal each other
A proportion is formed, to each one another

Solving a proportion, cross multiply and divide
The unknown value comes in for a slide

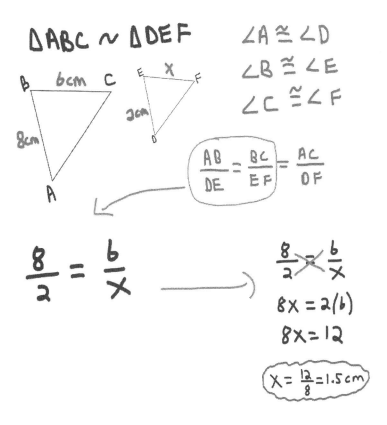

$\triangle ABC \sim \triangle DEF$

$\angle A \cong \angle D$
$\angle B \cong \angle E$
$\angle C \cong \angle F$

$$\frac{AB}{DE} = \frac{BC}{EF} = \frac{AC}{DF}$$

$$\frac{8}{2} = \frac{6}{x} \longrightarrow$$

$$\frac{8}{2} \times \frac{6}{x}$$

$$8x = 2(6)$$

$$8x = 12$$

$$x = \frac{12}{8} = 1.5 cm$$

Similar Triangles

A major topic in geometry
Is that of triangle similarity

Angles congruent, corresponding sides proportional
A powerful tool for anyone's arsenal

If two angles of two triangles congruent
Definitely similar, by Angle-Angle (AA) student

When corresponding sides are shown proportional
Side-Side-Side (SSS) is surely the way to go

Two sides proportional, between angle the same
Side-Angle-Side (SAS), similarity is named

Similar triangles have so many uses
Watch the lesson, be smart like Confucius

Triangle Proportionality Theorem

A line that intersects a triangle's two sides
Parallel to the third a proportionality ride

Divides the sides into proportional segments
Solve for the unknown, like your next birthday present

Set your up a ratio and make a proportion
Cross multiply and solve, no need for extortion

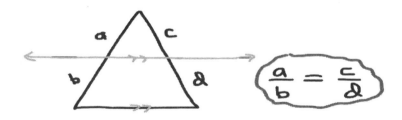

Angle Side Relationships

Angles across from congruent sides
Also congruent, no need to collide

When a side is larger than the other, though
So is the angle, across from the go

Pairs of triangles with two congruent sides
Angle between one's bigger inside

Side that's across from the larger one
Is also greater, oh so fun

Now don't forget before we're through
The converse of all I said is true

Pythagorean Inequalities

A squared plus B squared equals C squared
The Pythagorean Theorem has me scared

The sum of the legs to the power of two
Square root the result a hypotenuse for you

If the sum of the squares is more than squared C
The triangle is acute, look and see

When squared C is more than the sum of the others
An obtuse triangle comes in like our brother

When a, b & c come out as whole numbers
A Pythagorean triple will make you wonder

Don't forget the number one part
Check for a triangle before you start

Triangle inequality with three numbers
A possible triangle in case you slumber

Pythagorean Theorem Limerick

It's the Pythagorean Theorem
We really need to hear-em
A squared plus B squared equals C squared
A mathematical formula you'll be spared
Oh Pythagoras, really need to see him

Special Right Triangles

For right triangles with unknown sides
The Pythagorean Theorem will help you get by

But every now and then in certain cases
Special right triangles are off to the races

Shortcut avoiding the Pythagorean Theorem
We find unknown sides before you even see-em

The first one we have is the Isosceles Right
45-45-90, that's tight

Legs are congruent, this much is true
Hypotenuse found, times the square root of two

Next we have a 30-60-90
Unknown sides appear so shiny

Short leg half the hypotenuse
Give it a try or you have nothing to lose

Multiply short leg by the square root of three
You find the long leg, it's something to see

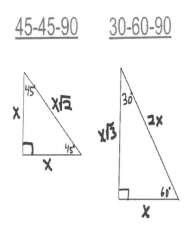

Angles of Elevation & Depression

The time has come for our next session
To learn about angles, elevation and depression

Looking forward horizontally
A zero angle, can't you see

When looking up and standing tall
Angle of elevation to the top of the wall

Staring down and feeling depressed
Angle of depression, you'll do your best

Above or below the horizontal line
Elevation or depression angles are fine

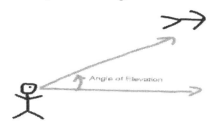

An angle of elevation is the angle
above the horizontal line of sight.

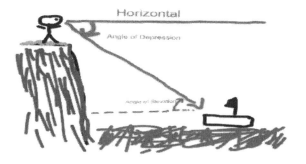

An angle of depression, is the angle
below the horizontal line of sight.

Area and Perimeter

A perimeter sums up all the sides
Distance around the shape applies

Area measures the space within
We use a formula to just begin

Parallelograms and rectangles base times height
To find the area and get it right

Trapezoids add the bases too
Multiply by the height and divide by two

Triangles, try to not get tangled
Half the base times height finagled

Kites and rhombi a special formula
Half the product of the diagonals I'm telling ya

So watch the examples and pay attention
Perimeter and area is our next lesson

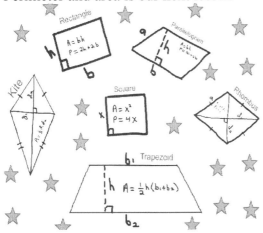

Regular Polygons

We're in the last quarter, the season is spring
Regular polygons will make you sing

A subtle word, not to take for granted
Call it regular and don't be left stranded

Congruent angles and congruent sides
A regular polygon surely coincides

An easy formula for finding perimeter
Number of sides times length, so sinister

It has an apothem, what a strange word
Distance from the center to the side is what I've heard

A Formula for area you really need to try
It's Half the apothem times the perimeter, don't cry

So sing-sing-sing, regular Polygons so loud
Learn about them, and make your teacher proud

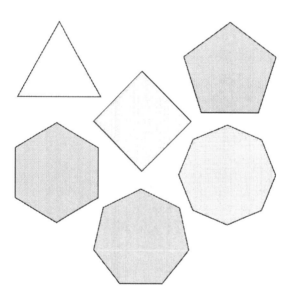

Composite Area

Formulas in geometry will get us through
For certain shapes we know them to

Triangles, rectangles, circles, and squares
Just find the formula, no need to care

But certain figures consist of shapes
Combined together as one so great

Composite shapes are what they're called
Geometric shapes put together that's all

Divide the shapes and find the areas
Add together, don't catch malaria

When finding areas in real life
Composite shapes will cause no strife

Composite Area by Subtraction

Sometimes a piece of the puzzle is missing
Composite area by subtraction no dissing

Just subtract the area of the shape
You'll find the shaded and feel so great

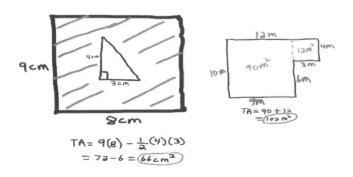

$TA = 9(8) - \frac{1}{2}(4)(3)$
$= 72 - 6 = \boxed{66 cm^2}$

$TA = 90 + 12$
$= \boxed{102 m^2}$

Geometric Probability

Total outcomes of possibility
Desired events in probability

A mathematical measurement of a given chance
Probability makes you sing and dance

Total outcomes in the sample space infinite
Geometric probability will keep you into it

Area of a shape or numbers on a line
Divided by the total if you'd be so inclined

Ratio of one onto another
Geometric probability so close like a brother

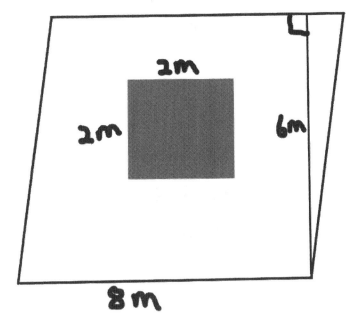

*What is the geometric probability that a random
 point selected within the parallelogram lies within
 the blue shaded area?

Geometric Solids

Prisms, cylinders, pyramids and cones
Geometric solids will take anyone home

Faces, edges and vertices
Three dimensional figures contain all of these

Formed by parallel congruent polygonal bases
Parallelogram sides are the prism's faces

Parallel, congruent, and bases circular
A cylinder formed, so extracurricular

Triangular faces at a common vertex
Polygonal bases in a pyramid circus

Time for ice cream two scoops in a cone
A circular base one vertex all alone

Named according to the shape of the base
A net can be formed to the shape, just in case

Learn the solids of geometry
Surface area and volume are coming to thee

*It's raining solids.

Surface Area

The base's perimeter times the height
The lateral surface, a rectangle that's right

To find the area of each base
Just use the formula for each special case

The lateral surface added to the bases
Total surface area and off to the races

You'll now know how much paint to order
To cover the surface, none left to the hoarder

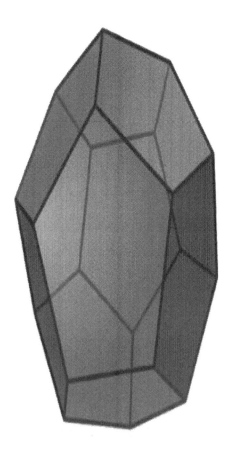

Lines that Intersect Circles

Now is time to come on board
For lines that are tangents, secants or chords

Touching the circle at just one point
We're off on a tangent line in the joint

A secant line just goes on through
Two points on the circle, it's nothing new

If on the circle the endpoints lay
The segments a chord, you're on the way

A chord going through a circle's center
Called a diameter, no need for a mentor

Radii congruent, circles are too
Concentric circles have same centers through

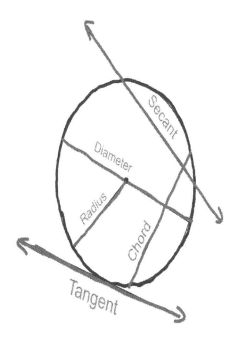

Arcs & Chords and Central Angles

At Central High we are so cool
We have an angle named for our school

A Central angle, yes it's called
Vertex center of a circle, that's all

It intercepts a circle's arc
Both major and minor just for starts

Central angle, it's arc does measure
The minor one is no less treasured

Congruent angles, Congruent chords
Converse also in accord

Arcs and chords and central angles
One pair congruent, the others tango

A radius perpendicular to a chord
Surely bisects, there's more in store

Do the work and hear the lesson
Like Hidden Figures, space flight not messing

Sector Area & Arc Length

A piece of pie, a circle's sector
Another portion for the next lecture

A portion of the circle's whole
Sector area or arc length told

Central angle over 360
Times the area or circumference nifty

Sector area and old arc length
The source of all my geometric strength

Inscribed Angles

Vertex on the circle's edge
An inscribed angle placed on the ledge

It measures half the circle's arc
Or central angle on my mark

An arc subtending half around
Inscribed angle is right on down

Congruent arcs congruent angles
Whether inscribed or centrally entangled

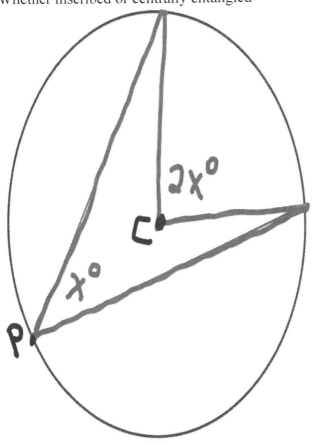

Slope Haiku

Rise over the run
Slope of a line, doing fine
Please don't step on me

Quadrilaterals

Quadrilateral, a planar shape
Four angles and sides will not escape

They come in many shapes and forms
According to name, I could've sworn

First one called a parallelogram
One that's wanted by Uncle Sam

Opposite sides are parallel
They're also congruent from what I tell

Adjacent angles supplementary
Opposite ones congruency

Diagonals are another sect
I'll tell you now they do bisect

Parallelogram with congruent sides
Called a rhombus, I wouldn't lie

Its diagonals are perpendicular
Ninety-degree angle, spectacular

Parallelogram, angles congruent
Called a rectangle, for my students

Its diagonals are congruent too
Good to know, but we're not through

Next one others call a square
Like Mr. H who has no hair

Four congruent sides and angles
It's both a rhombus and a rectangle

Another quadrilateral called a Kite
Not a parallelogram, that is right

Congruent adjacent sides for flight
It flies so high, it's out of sight

Perpendicular diagonals make its shape
So much fun, we'll all go ape

Last one called an Isosceles Trapezoid
Two parallel sides not to avoid

Legs congruent, base angles to
That is all, and now we're through

Quadrilateral	Properties	
Rectangle	4 right angles and opposite sides equal	
Square	4 right angles and 4 equal sides	
Parallelogram	Two pairs of parallel sides and opposite sides equal	
Rhombus	Parallelogram with 4 equal sides	
Trapezoid	Two sides are parallel	
Kite	Two pairs of adjacent sides of the same length	

Thanksgiving

Hey there students, I'd just like to say
Hope your school year is going okay

We've reached a milestone, yes it's true
Tomorrow is Thanksgiving, no feeling blue

Time off to spend with friends and family
Reconnecting with Uncle Stanley

Forget all your troubles and problems today
It's time to be thankful, at least for the day

So take some time off, and have some fun
Do a little homework, a balance is won

See you next Monday when the time off is through
Bright and early and ready for school

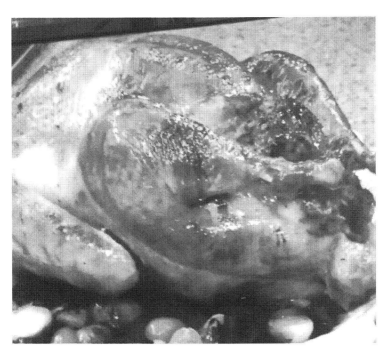

Functions from Graphical Shapes

Identifying functions can be done
Their graphical shapes are how they run

Linear, you may just know about
Graph runs straight, there is no doubt

Quadratic functions, a special call
Running along the path of a ball

Exponential Growth starts so slow
More and more upward, increasing they grow

Decaying exponential, a graphical understanding
Very steep decent to the runway for landing

One more shape to learn this hour
A function full of strength and power

Monomial term with positive exponent
Classified power at that moment

Shape of graph concave up or down
Positive real gives domain all around

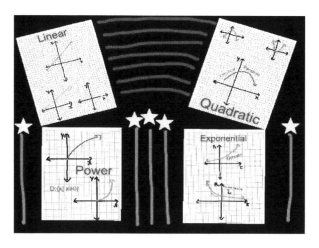

Functions from Numerical Patterns

If graphical analysis makes you unstable
Then learn the functions by looking at tables

It's linear, it's linear, can't you see
An add-add pattern, so tabularly

An add-multiply pattern, no need to sigh
It's exponential please, just give it a try

Last but not least, so powerfully elite
A multiply-multiply pattern so mighty, so sweet

Logarithmic Functions

Ready or not, let's get in rhythm
Exponential inverses are called logarithms

Inverse of the exponential function
Reflection of its graph in conjunction

Multiply-add so says the table
A pattern from the logarithmic playbook

Exponential written in logarithmic form
Convert it back, it will conform

The base of a log, is the base of the exponent
It helps you convert at any moment

Solving equations called exponential
Knowing your logs, absolutely essential

There's so much more in the lesson to see
Please pay attention so carefully

Properties of logarithms

To master the logs and do it in style
Knowing the properties will make you smile

A log of a product is the sum of the logs
A useful property for this old dog

A log of a quotient, the difference of logs
You need to know, to get through the fog

Log of X to a power?
Exponent out front this very hour

When base of log and exponent are equal
You have an argument for our next sequel

The log of one equals zero
Yes it's one, our true hero

$$\text{If } Log_b X = Y$$

$$\text{Then } b^y = X$$

$$Log\, XY = Log X + Log Y$$

$$Log\frac{X}{Y} = Log X - Log Y$$

$$Log\, X^n = n\, Log X$$

$$\text{If } A^x = B$$

$$\text{Then } X = \frac{Log B}{Log A}$$

Line of Best Fit

Nearing the end, can barely sit
Learning lines of data's best fit

Plotting points of data pairs
Look for a trend, take time and stare

Falling in line with a positive slope
A one correlation, please take note

A downward trend, makes you wonder
Correlation negative, one down under

Lines that go through all the points
Called best fit throughout the joint

Sometimes lines don't touch them all
The best fit one is closest yawl

Vertical distance from point to the line
Called a residual of the least, so inclined

The residual squares whose sum is at least
A line of best fit comes in bringing peace

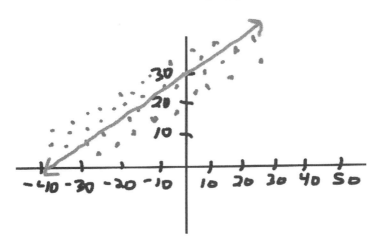

Exponential Functions

Domain variable itself is an exponent
Called exponential from that moment

The base of the exponent, a multiplier, see
According to whatever the exponent be

In today's lesson we'll direct our study
To a base called e, the natural log's buddy

Its graph increases naturally
Like any exponential that we see

Compound interest also exponential
Continuous compounding base e is essential

Take one plus the rate divided by the compounding number
Raised to the power of the number and time it was under

This is the percentage the principal has grown
You now can reap what you've previously sewn

So listen carefully to the lesson ahead
Learn exponentials, that's what I said

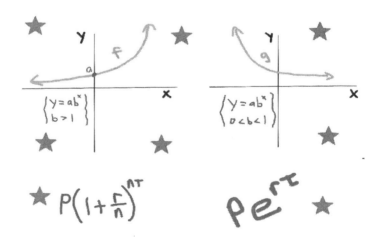

Domain and Range

Domain and Range sound so strange
Just mere words with an unpleasant ring

Just take the X value all the way
That's the way Domain is played

If you get a Y, very nice try
It's in the Range, the output is why

If you have a graph, that's alright
Domain is displayed from left to right

From the graph it's also true
The range will cover from the ground up through

If you use a function that's Insane
Undefined values never enter the Domain

From the Domain into the function
Out to the Range in conjunction

So domain and range are not so bad,
Give it a try, you'll be so glad

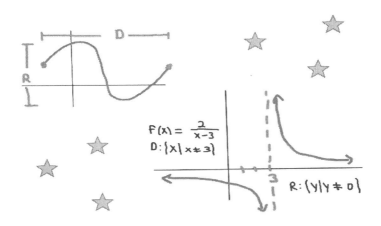

$$F(x) = \frac{2}{x-3}$$
$$D: \{x | x \neq 3\}$$

$$R: \{y | y \neq 0\}$$

What's a Function?

What's a function? It's just another word
It takes it from the domain, that is what I've heard

For every input out from the domain
Is just one output, a function is the same

A vertical line hits the graph at just one point
They say it's a function, even in the joint

Horizontal works for one-to-one too
If it touches two points, it doesn't come true

What's a function, I think I understand
For every Input, one output is just grand

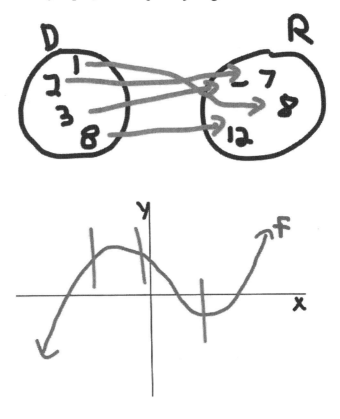

Transformations

Transformations are scary, so I've heard
Really nothing, just a fancy sounding word

Horizontal phase shifts the graph left or right
Inside the function, opposite in sight

For vertical shift, subtract or add the number
Up or down by the value, don't slumber

Stretching horizontally by a factor?
Multiply the input by the reciprocal for stature

To stretch the graph up-and-down, don't you see
Multiply the output by a constant doe rae me

So forget every little thing you've heard
Transformation is not a scary word

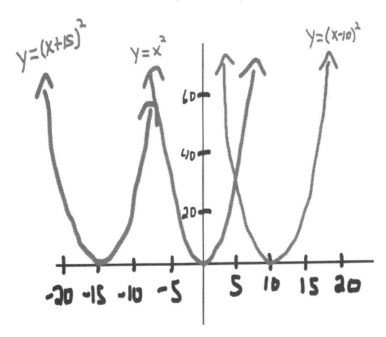

Transformations Two

Transformations move a graph all around
Sometimes they change the shape, pretty sound

Adding to the input, horizontally to the left
Subtracting the same shifts right, so I checked

Shifting the graph up or down?
Apply a constant all around

To reflect a graph, over the X axis
Multiply the function by a negative, like our taxes

Now if you want to reflect, over the Y
Input negative X and give it a try

Stretching a graph can be monumental
Along the vertical or the horizontal

To stretch a graph vertically
Multiply the function by a constant, don't you see

Stretching a function in a horizontal manner
Multiply the input by the reciprocal that's a matter

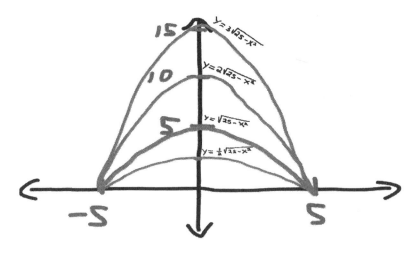

Functions and Graphs Two

For Zeros of a function, this is all you do
Find an old x-value, that outputs nothing too

Increasing /decreasing functions should not make you blue
Read the graph from left to right is all you have to do

If the graph is rising,
increasing's not surprising

A graph that is on its way on down
Decreasing is what we call it now

Relative min or maximum
Could frighten the very best of them

But it's okay, not to fray
Listen to what I have to say

A relative max is higher up
Then all the points around its stuff

For relative min, this is true
It's lower than all that's in its hue

Even or Odd functions, here is the test
Input negative X, I'll explain the rest

If the output is the same as what you started trying
We call the function even, no need for all the crying

If the function's odd like your teacher, Mr. H,
Output is the negative of the function, just in case

Combinations of Functions

A function combo's not a tricky thing
Just combine like terms, or multiplying

Instead of inputting to the functions separately
We can put them together into one especially

Don't forget some common rules too
You need to know before we get through

Combining like terms, this will get you through
Combine the coefficients, it's nothing you can't do

A monomial product is not so bad
Just multiply coefficients, the exponents add

Combining functions using all the operators
Just one function, something truly greater

A composition function is another thing
You need to learn it now, before the bell will ring

Instead of inputting just another number
We place a function on the inside of the other

If you want to find the domain of a composite
First look at the inner functions closest

Don't forget that it's sometimes true
The outer function may have restrictions too

Well that is it for our poem today
Time for the lesson, hear what I say

Inverse Functions

The study of functions is not complete
Without an inverse, very sweet

To find an inverse this is all you do,
Interchange the input with the output too

So if we have Y as a function of X
Just interchange them, I'll explain the rest

Solve for Y, it's all you must do,
Just give it a try, it's part of school

What you have is the inverse function
You can use it now in conjunction

Another way to find the inverse, say
It's from the function's graphical display

Just reflect the graph over the 45 line
It's Y equals X, you'll do just fine

We're not done yet unless we mention
The inverse test through compositions

Composing a function and inverse?
Out comes X, The rest is in the next verse

If we go the other way it's found
The inverse of the function gives X all around

So listen carefully and you'll do so great
This lesson is brought by your teacher, Mr. H

Probability

A mathematical way to measure chance
Probability, will you take the stance?

It's all about counting, see
The number of elements for you and me

Count the outcomes for the desired event
Divide by the total and pay the rent

When there are no outcomes that are desired
The probability is zero that you'll be hired

But when the desired equals the total possible
A probability of one makes you unstoppable

Counting Principles

Oh so many outcomes, more than I can see
I need to count them, please oh please help me

Mutually exclusive, events not overlapping
No conflicting schedules, feel like going camping

Events that are independent, this is always true
Whatever is the outcome, has no affect on you

A and B, two events, each occur in sequence
Multiply the outcomes of each of them for frequents

Keywords: and, then, or both
Tell us to multiply, you'll count like a coach

Then there's that other key word: or
Add them together and head for the door

This is a poem of riddles and mysteries
Let the lesson unfold and make sense of these, please

Probability Permutations

Counting methods in probability
Permutations are one for thee

An ordered arrangement of various things
You'll count so fast, heads will swing

Apply the multiplication principle, it's one of the ways
You'll find the permutations, it's what I say

License plates and telephone numbers
Permutations will make you wonder

An ordered election of rank and file
Permutations will make you smile

So listen to the lesson carefully
Permutations will make thee glee

Probability Combinations

Another kind of counting method
Unranked choice, don't be trepid

Order doesn't really matter
Nothing makes me feel gladder

Call it a combo or combination
It's a way of counting, a new sensation

Divide the repetitions from the permutations
It's how we do it in a mathematics nation

For dinners or entrées or pizza toppings
Combinations will make thee sing

So it doesn't really matter how it's put together
Using combinations will make it even better

Properties of Probability

To find the probability of two events
It helps to know if they are dependent

When they are dependent, this is so true
The probability changes all the way through

Two events that happen together
We call it an intersection, it doesn't get better

It's a probability of A times a probability of B
Don't forget the dependency

To find the probability of either or
Sum them up, your only chore

Call it a union, if not mutually exclusive
Subtract the intersection, nothing intrusive

Complementary events, A or not A
They add up to one, making it okay

So listen to the teacher 'til the lesson is through
There's much more probability waiting for you

$$P(A \vee B) = P(A) + P(B) - P(A \wedge B)$$

$$P(A \wedge B) = P(A) \cdot P(B)$$

$$P(A \mid B) = \frac{P(A \wedge B)}{P(B)}$$

Probability Haiku

Probability
You must learn to count numbers
Chance of snow tonight

Random Variables

Come to the trial, random chance involved
X out of N successes, probability must be solved

Outcomes of each trial can succeed or fail
A Binomial Distribution tells no tales

X out of N successes for the outcome
Many ways to count, and then some

Combinations count the number of ways
That X out of N can be played

Don't forget about success and failure
Raised to the power of their frequency tailored

Whoever thought math was so cool?
We get to do poetry while learning in school

Mathematical Expectation

Predicting an outcome by mathematical means
Mathematical expectation appears on the scene

A game of chance, is the advantage mine?
Expecting dollars, or losing, fine

A new sensation, with appreciation
Using probability for expectation

Multiply the probabilities by the outcome score
Add them together, I will say no more

An expected value or weighted average
You'll know the outcome before the damage

Another example of the use of mathematics
Helps us understand the probability of our status

Polynomials

A Monomial is a single term, defined for all real numbers
Two, three or more together make a poly we don't wonder

If you add up all the exponents of a monomial term
You end up with its degree, no need to be concerned

A Polynomial's degree, as far as I can see
Equals to the highest monomial degree

The next thing that we do, it's really up to you
We need to write the poly, in standard form too

Order terms from greatest, to the least degree
Standard form is not formidable, you'll see

Oh Polynomial, our beloved friend
It is great to know you, true to the end

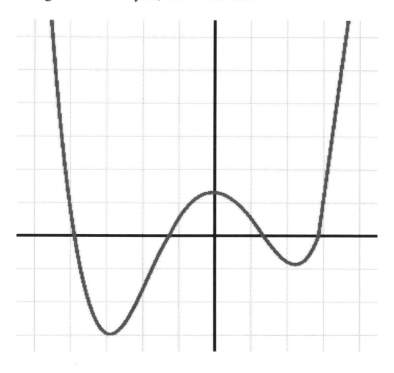

Dividing Polynomials

Time to increase our mathematical vision
A step-by-step process called polynomial division

First term of the divisor into the first term of the dividend
You'll place the term in a moment's end

Multiply, subtract, and bring down the term
Repeat the process, don't be concerned

When you run out of terms to bring down
Your quotient and remainder will be there sound

So listen to the lesson and what I say
Do all your work, it'll be okay

$$
\begin{array}{r}
x^3 + 2x^2 - 3x + 1 \\
3x-2\overline{\smash{\big)}\,3x^4 + 4x^3 - 13x^2 + 9x + 3} \\
-(3x^4 - 2x^3) \\
\hline
6x^3 - 13x^2 \\
-(6x^3 - 4x^2) \\
\hline
-9x^2 + 9x \\
-(-9x^2 + 6x) \\
\hline
3x + 3 \\
-(3x - 2) \\
\hline
5
\end{array}
$$

$$
x^3 + 2x^2 - 3x + 1 + \frac{5}{3x-2}
$$

Quadratic Functions

A monomial is a single term, defined for all real numbers
Two, three or more together make a poly we don't wonder

A special type of polynomial, we would like to study
We call it a quadratic, in math it's our best buddy

Let "a,b,c" be real numbers with "a" not equal zero
Then "a-x- squared plus b-x-plus c," make a quadratic function hero

A quadratic has a special graph, its shape is called a parabola
It opens up or downward, by the sign of "a," no babbla

The vertex is the highest point when the graph opens downward
But when it opens upward it's the lowest forever onward

The axis of symmetry, a vertical line cutting the shape in half
If you plot the points on one side, you'll know the other's path

Transformations, another tool that help us sketch the graphs
Just start with old x squared, and transform it just like that

A vertex form of the parabola consists of transformations
Coming from the origin, using horizontal and vertical translations

If you know the vertex of the parabola, with a point that is on it
You can find the equation using vertex form
No need to try and con it

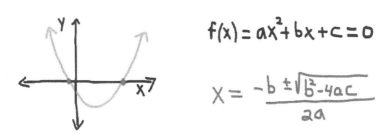

$$f(x) = ax^2 + bx + c = 0$$

$$x = \frac{-b \pm \sqrt{b^2 - 4ac}}{2a}$$

Remainder Theorem

Today we learn to find a remainder
Without dividing, were not in danger

Input a number into the equation
Output a remainder, quite the sensation

Applying skills of synthetic substitution
Higher education of the math institution

Dividing polynomials by X -C
F of C gives the remainder for thee

Have a good day and listen to the lesson
Increase your knowledge, it is your blessing

Synthetic Division

When we divide by linear factors of coefficient one
Use synthetic division and have some fun

First write the polynomial in standard form
Synthetic division, we will conform

Put the coefficients down on paper
Line underneath for your next caper

Place the number in the box
From the divisor, Opposites rock

Bringing down the first coefficient
Multiplied by the number, very efficient

Multiply add, all the way
You get the remainder at the end of the day

Numbers you end up with when you're through
Coefficients of a polynomial, a degree less than you

Binomial Expansion Theorem

Expanding binomials to higher powers
Binomial theorem comes into the hour

Take a moment and look at the exponent
It's the row of the triangle, a crucial component

These are the coefficients of all the terms
They'll get you started without concern

Combinations from probability
Give Pascal's triangle for all to see

The expansion uses Pascal's coefficients
Term by term, so very efficient

First and second term in the binomial
Raised to a power, why did I not know

One of the exponents decreases each term
The other increases, this we can learn

Just remember within the expansion
Each term's degree is constant, no bashing

The last part you do is simplify
It'll get easier if you give it a try

$$(x+y)^4 = {}_4C_0(x)^4(y)^0 + {}_4C_1(x)^3(y)^1 + {}_4C_2(x)^2(y)^2 + {}_4C_3(x)^1(y)^3 + {}_4C_4(x)^0(y)^4$$

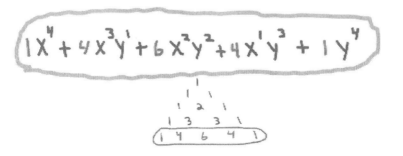

$$1x^4 + 4x^3y^1 + 6x^2y^2 + 4x^1y^3 + 1y^4$$

$$
\begin{array}{ccccccc}
& & & 1 & & & \\
& & 1 & & 1 & & \\
& 1 & & 2 & & 1 & \\
1 & & 3 & & 3 & & 1 \\
1 & & 4 & & 6 & & 4 & & 1
\end{array}
$$

Complex Numbers

Tried to square root a negative number
It didn't work, I begin to wonder

Using all my imagination
To get me through this complete stagnation

Mathematicians invented the number 'i'
Square root of -1, why oh why?

Solving equations with imaginary solutions
It works for real life, what a revolution

Just take the square root like you normally do
Place the 'i' and then you're through

What you have is a complex number
Use your imagination, no need to wonder

Descartes' Rule of Signs

Positive or negative polynomial roots
Descartes' rule for the young and astute

Just count the sign changes for F of X
How many positive roots? It's in the test

It's equal to the number of reversals in sign
Or an even number less, let's get to the grind

For negative roots, the same is true
With input negative X, and simplified through

Descartes' rule is fun for all
Positive or negative roots, your next call

Rational Roots Theorem

Determining possible roots that are rational
Rational roots theorem has gone international

Leading coefficient and constant term factors
Write them down, and be a transactor

Constant term factors, call them p
q is the leading coefficiency

It's the ratio of p divided by q
Possible rational roots are there for you

Test them out using synthetic substitution
If the remainder's zero, you're close to the solution

Continue the process 'til you reach a quadratic
Then use the formula, nothing erratic

Watch the lesson and listen too
Rational Roots Theorem, we love you

$f(x) = 2x^3 - 5x^2 + 4x - 1$

$$P: \pm 1$$

$$q: \pm 1 \ \pm 2$$

$$\frac{P}{q}: \pm\frac{1}{1} \ \pm\frac{1}{2}$$

$$\underline{1|} \ \ 2 \ -5 \ \ 4 \ -1$$
$$\ \ \ \ \ \ \ \ \ \ \ \ 2 \ -3 \ \ 1$$
$$\overline{\ \ \ \ \ \ 2 \ -3 \ \ 1 \ \ \ 0}$$

$$(x-1)(2x^2-3x+1)$$

$$\boxed{(x-1)(2x-1)(x-1)}$$

71

Imaginary and Irrational Roots Theorem

Don't be irrational, and try to imagine
Imaginary and irrational roots at the cabin

It's said they come in conjugate pairs
Just change the sign, no need to care

a +bi, oh so complex
a - bi, a conjugate next

Did you know it's also true?
Irrational numbers have conjugates too

Any roots complex or irrational
Have conjugate pairs, oh so rational

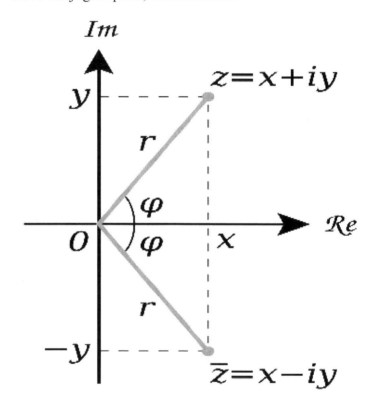

Graphical Shapes

Today we study shapes of graphs
Pay close attention, it goes sort of fast

Start by observing the degree of the poly
No reason for students to feel melancholy

The number of turns, one less than the degree
I'll show you some pictures, so you can see

Degree also determines the end behavior
Of the polynomial, no need to show favor

If the degree is even, same on both ends
When it's odd, they're opposite then

It's all according to the function's degree
Listen to the lesson so carefully

Function's End Behavior

When the degree is odd, leading coefficient positive
A down-up pattern is very provocative

Leading coefficient negative? Flip the function over
An up-down pattern like a four-leaf clover

Even degree functions, with a positive leading
An up-up pattern will leave you pleading

Even degree, leading negative
A down-down pattern, no need for a sedative

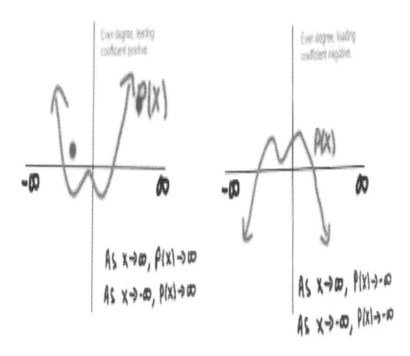

Even degree, leading coefficent positive.

$P(x)$

As $x \to \infty$, $P(x) \to \infty$

As $x \to -\infty$, $P(x) \to \infty$

Even degree, leading coefficent negative.

$P(x)$

As $x \to \infty$, $P(x) \to -\infty$

As $x \to -\infty$, $P(x) \to -\infty$

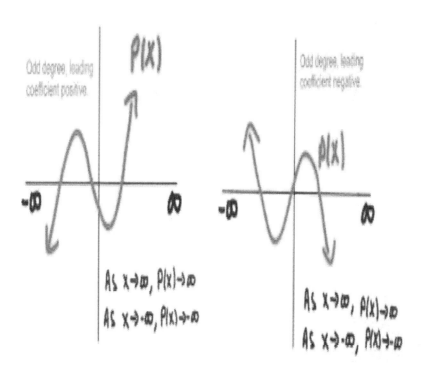

Odd degree, leading coefficient positive.

$P(x)$

As $x \to \infty$, $P(x) \to \infty$

As $x \to -\infty$, $P(x) \to -\infty$

Odd degree, leading coefficient negative.

$P(x)$

As $x \to \infty$, $P(x) \to \infty$

As $x \to -\infty$, $P(x) \to \infty$

Horizontal Asymptotes

Another type of end behavior
For rational functions, tell your neighbor

It's neither up, nor is it down
Comes in level without a sound

Call this behavior asymptotic
It's horizontal, hope you got it

Horizontal line drawn with dashes
Y = k, its equation smashes

Degree of bottom, greater than top
Y = 0, no need to stop

Numerator and denominator, degrees are equal
Leading coefficients will lead the sequel

Just take the ratio of the two
Horizontal equation gets you through

If the numerator's degree is greater though
No horizontal asymptotes, time to go

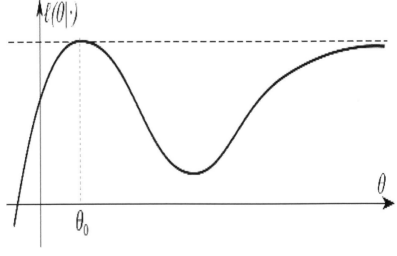

Vertical Asymptotes

Where rational functions are undefined
Vertical asymptotes are easy to find

Equations of form x = k
Vertical dashed line is what I say

One thing that is always true
The function's graph will not go through

It either approaches up or down
Positive or negative infinity bound

Another thing we must see
Odd or even, the asymptote's degree

Even degree, say with pride
Graph approaches same on both sides

If graph turns in opposite directions
Degree is odd to my recollection

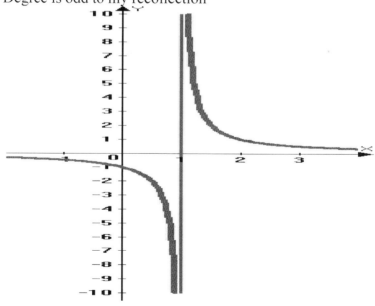

Rapid Curve Sketching

It's time to put it all together
Rapid curve sketching before the weather

We need to determine the asymptotes
Horizontal and vertical, take good notes

Next we go to quite the depth
To find the curve's Y-intercept

Don't forget about the roots
Where Numerator is zero in cahoots

Odd or even we must check
Vertical asymptotes and roots on deck

Now we have the information
To graph the curve in formation

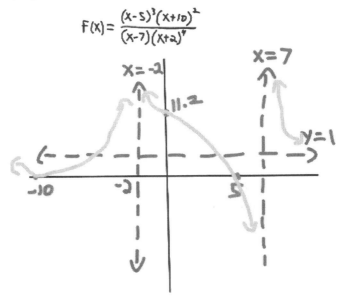

$$F(x) = \frac{(x-5)^3(x+10)^2}{(x-7)(x+2)^4}$$

VA: X=7 odd   Roots: X=5   HA: Y= 1   Yint ≈ 11.2
X= -2 even   X= -10

78

Winter Break

It's the last day of the academic year
Students everywhere have begun to cheer

It's winter vacation and holiday time
Together with family to wine and dine

Playing outside and having some fun
No homework or deadlines need to be done

After the holidays, bring in the new year
Just a couple of days, and you'll be back here

Make a resolution pertaining to school
You're an all-star, this year you rule

See you all back when the break is through
Safe and sound and ready for school

Standard Position Angle

When taking geometry, we classified angles
Acute, obtuse or right for the tango

But now we look from a whole new way
We form an angle by rotating a ray

Starting the rotation initially
Rotation ends so terminally

Turn counterclockwise, a positive direction
Rotating clockwise to the negative section

Make the initial the positive x-axis
A standard position for doing our taxes

Terminal side in one of four quadrants
Forms a reference for our next convent

Acute angle formed with the x
A reference angle comes up next

We now know a thing about standard position
Angles turned from the positive x mission

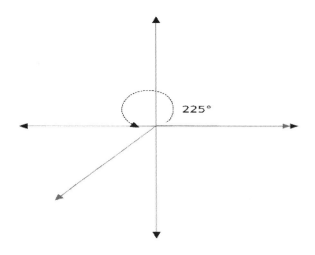

Inverse Trig Ratios

Inverse trig is what we use
When finding angles, it's what we choose

Inverse functions remember, please
Output to input it's one of these

Trig of Any Angle

Now that we've learned about standard position
Trig of any angle is our next mission

Given a point on the terminal side
The six trig ratios come in like the tide

First we sketch a triangle for reference
With X and Y for legs, in essence

Hypotenuse found by Pythagorean Theorem
Trig ratios stand out, we now clearly see-em

Legs of the triangle positive or negative
According to its coordinates, no need to be tentative

Don't forget the special right tri's
We find exact values, try not to cry

All students take calculus, quite the phrase
Positive or negative trig values will daze

If we know the trig angle's ratio
We find the reference of the angle in case though

Reference angle in two different quadrants
According to the sign of the trig ratio's squadron

Circular Functions

Around the circle the trig functions go
Values repeated so cyclically so

Length of the cycle is called the period
Applications varied so infinite and myriad

Y is the sine and X is the cose
Y over X is the tangent, we boast

Two pie radians all the way around
Trigonometric functions are circular bound

Graphing Sine & Cosine

A thing with trig not to avoid
Is graphing shapes of sinusoids

The Sine and Cosine's basic shape
The unit circle sets it straight

Cosine is X and sine is Y
From the circle let it fly

Repeated shape across the domain
Period is the length of the cycle's reign

Halfway through the max and min
Sinusoidal axis called within

The graph it has an amplitude
Middle to the max or min it's true

Horizontal or vertical transformal shift
Graphs of sinusoids set adrift

Don't forget the transformations
For stretching functions across the nation

Secant & Cosecant

Cosine and sine, we've sketched the graphs
Time for reciprocals, we're here at last

Where the sinusoid is equal zero
Reciprocal graph is asymptotic like Nero

They have no roots, and behave periodic
360 degrees repeatedly robotic

Alternating pattern throughout the domain
Cosecant and secant look much the same

Graph of Tangent

Now that we've graphed sine and cosine
Graph of tangent falls into line

Tangents the ratio of Y to X
Sine over cosine an identical jest

Don't forget where X is zero
Vertical asymptotes come in like heroes

Roots are fine, they come from sine
It's where it's zero, all the time

Plot the roots and asymptotes
You'll get the graph, so take good notes

Periodic function of 180 degrees
Repeated shape of graphical ease

When graphing cotangent it's truly insane
Just take the reciprocal and do the same

ArcCosine

The principal branch of the cosine function
Zero to pi, its domain in conjunction

Truly invertible as we'll see
Called the Arccosine for you and for me

A cosine's argument we need to find
To solve the equation and be on time

Take plus or minus the cosine inverse
Plus multiples of two pi to conquer the universe

Oh, arccosine, a fancy sounding word
Simply an inverse, that's what I've heard

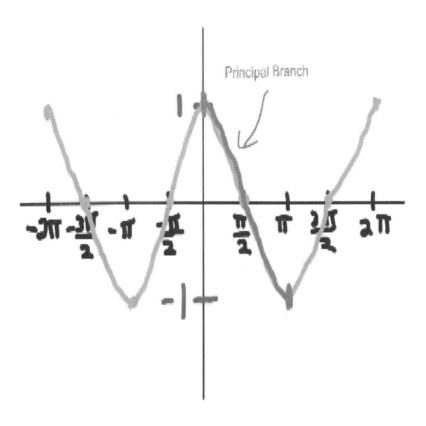

Unit Circle

Hey everyone, let's have some fun
The unit circle has a radius of one

It is very useful as you'll see
We use it a lot in trigonometry

The terminal side crosses the circle at a spot
You'll find the trig values, you're getting hot

The cosine equals the X value, please
The Y value gives the sine for thee

If you want to find the tangent too
Y over X will get you through

It's also great for special angles
You can find trig values, no calculator to wrangle

So listen to the lesson carefully
It's time to dig deeper, fundamentally

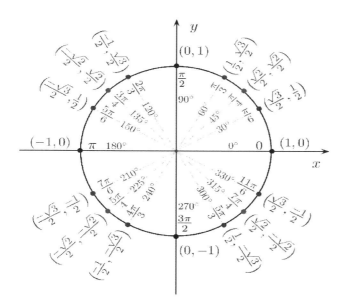

SOH-CAH-TOA

SOH-CAH-TOA is what they say
Memorizing trig ratios, it's one of the ways

The sine is the opposite over the hypotenuse
That's the SOH, in case you're confused

Cosine is the CAH, let's set it straight
It's the adjacent over the hypotenuse, it feels so great

Now is time for the tangent TOA
Let's knock it down, like Rocky Balboa

The tangent is the opposite over the adjacent
That's where the TOA comes in for replacement

So memorize your trig ratios, won't you please
You can do it, it'll be a breeze

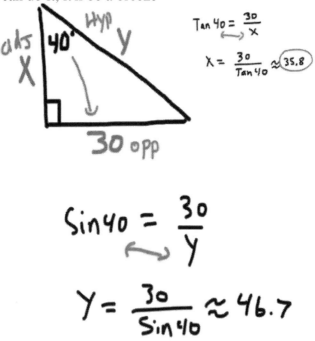

$$\text{Tan } 40 = \frac{30}{x}$$

$$x = \frac{30}{\text{Tan } 40} \approx 35.8$$

$$\text{Sin } 40 = \frac{30}{y}$$

$$y = \frac{30}{\text{Sin } 40} \approx 46.7$$

Trig on the Circle

If you want to find trig ratios of any angle too
Learn standard position to help you on through

Just make the initial side, the positive X
Rotate counterclockwise, make that your next text

The acute angle formed with the terminal side and X axis,
It's called a reference angle, even in Texas

A reference triangle is what you use
To find trig values, nothing to lose

Make a reference triangle, from your reference angle
You can now find all trig values, no need to get tangled

One more thing before we get through
Something you don't want to forget to do

The legs of your triangle can be positive or negative
According to their direction, no need for a sedative

So pay careful attention to your lesson from the teach
I just can't wait, so ready to preach

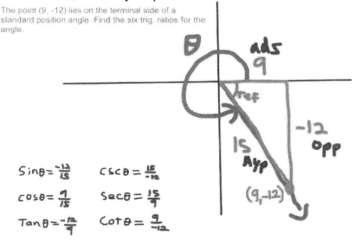

The point (9, -12) lies on the terminal side of a standard position angle. Find the six trig. ratios for the angle.

$$\sin\theta = \tfrac{-12}{15} \qquad \csc\theta = \tfrac{15}{-12}$$

$$\cos\theta = \tfrac{9}{15} \qquad \sec\theta = \tfrac{15}{9}$$

$$\tan\theta = \tfrac{-12}{9} \qquad \cot\theta = \tfrac{9}{-12}$$

Radians and Degrees

Like different units of measure, when it comes to length
Angles in degrees or radians, the source of all my strength

360 increments all the way around
Each a measure one degree, a system pretty sound

Circle's arclength divided by the radius
You have a radian angle, no need to be the brainiest

Converting an angle from radians to degrees
180 divided by pie, no time to even sneeze

For degrees to radians, this is all you do
Take pie divided by 180, and multiply on through

So this is how you do it, but there may be more to see
Pay attention closely to the lesson in front of thee

Angular and Linear Velocity

Rotational speed of an angle turning
Radians or degrees per unit time burning

Translates into a linear speed
Just multiply by the radius in radians, please

Two wheels connected by a chain or a string
Linear speed is the same we'll sing

Transmission factor is the ratio of size
One wheel to the other, an angular prize

Angular and linear velocity so cool
Truly connected, we learn it in school

Double Angle Formulas

Double angle formulas for sine and cosine
A single-one argument for the angle that's fine

Sine of a double angle 2X
Two Sine, Cosine of the single angle next

That's not all, we're not through
Unless we talk about the cosine too

Cosine squared minus the sine squared, see
Cosine double angle is the best for me

Two sine squared of x minus one
Or one minus two cosine squared just for fun

These are the double angles for sine and cosine
Please don't forget, you'll do just fine

$$\sin 2\theta = 2\sin\theta\cos\theta$$

$$\cos 2\theta = \cos^2\theta - \sin^2\theta$$

$$= 1 - 2\sin^2\theta$$

or

$$= 2\cos^2\theta - 1$$

Law of Sines

Please listen now, and don't be awed
Ignorance is no excuse for breaking the law

In this world we have many rules
The Law of Sines will make you so cool

The sign of the angle over the opposite side
Is always the same, no matter which ones you try

Knowing the angle and the opposite side too
The law of sines is there just for you

To find the area of an oblique triangle
Take half the two sides times the sine of the between angle

Listen to the lesson very carefully through
Please follow the law, it's what we do

$$\frac{\sin A}{a} + \frac{\sin B}{b} + \frac{\sin C}{c}$$

$$\frac{a}{\sin A} + \frac{b}{\sin B} + \frac{c}{\sin C}$$

Trigonometric Equations

Trigonometric equations of a fundamental nature
Solved using techniques of an algebraic stature

Isolating the function to just one side
All by itself, an argument subsides

All Students Take Calculus, is what I've heard
Positive or negative trig values are so absurd

Knowing the quadrant the reference angle lies
According to the sign of the trig ratios ties

All students take calculus, what a phrase
Placing reference angles, that's the next phase

Use the proper quadrants for each reference angle
You'll find the solutions with the reference triangle

If you know the period, all the better
Add multiples to the solution for an infinite letter

Ex: Sketch the following sinusoid using a degree
scale , then sketch again using a radian scale.

$$y = 4\cos 5x$$

$$\text{Period} = \frac{360}{5} = 72$$

$$\text{or } \frac{2\pi}{5}$$

$$\text{Amp} = 4$$

Period divided by 4 gives the
horizontal scale for the graph

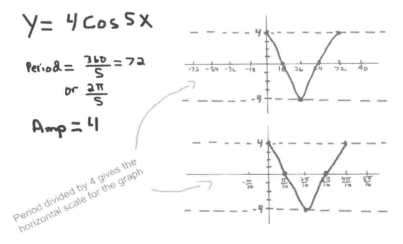

91

Law of Cosines

In this day of rules and regulations
Follow the law for mathematical situations

A certain law keeps you out of trouble
The Law of Cosines will break through the rubble

Knowing two sides and the angle in-between
The law of cosines most certainly can be seen

Also true if you know three sides
To find an angle, Law of Cosines applies

The square of a side is the sum of the squares of the others
Minus 2 times the cosine of the between angle's mother

Heron's formula will get you through
For finding area, this is for you

Determine the semi-perimeter "s"
Now I'm going to tell you the rest

Find three values by subtracting the sides
From the semi perimeter, just give it a try

Multiply the three values by the semi perimeter
Then take the square root, nothing so sinister

You have the area, why even cry
Just by knowing the perimeter and sides

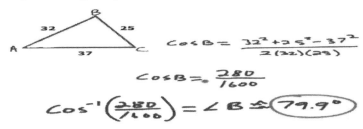

Graphs of Sine and Cosine

Today we get to learn okay,
Graphing the sine and the cosine way

First we find the amplitude
So please don't get an attitude.

It's half the difference between the max and min
Or from the mid-value, no need to sin

Horizontal shift times 360 or two-pi
Period of the function is right there, so don't cry

Horizontal scale is the period over four
Add it to the phase shift, to start the graph and more

Upper and lower limits? This is what you do
Apply the amplitude to the middle value, too

Now Sine and Cosine each have a pattern
Like the beautiful rings of our sixth planet, Saturn

Middle max, middle min
Pattern of sine, we're here to win

Max middle, min middle
Cosine's patterns like playing a fiddle

Now put it all together and sketch the graph
A beautiful sinusoid is here at last

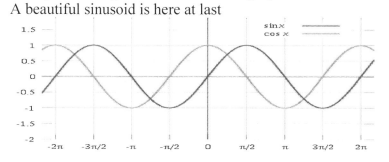

Limits

Listen to the lesson, hear what I say
Something is approaching, it's on its way

It gets infinitely close to a certain number
It's called a limit, no time to slumber

Functions not approaching a value insist
No such limit shall ever exist

It must approach the same number from both sides
Or the limit won't exist, a wasted ride

Unbounded behavior, oh so true
There is no limit for me or for you

So let's behave well and come together
Let's hear the lesson, and forget about the weather

Properties of Limits

Please listen carefully, can't believe my sight
Something's approaching from the left and the right

It never arrives, but gets infinitely closer
To the limit value, my brain is a toaster

In today's lesson, we'll learn a thing or two
Evaluating limits is what I'll teach you

Our friend the polynomial, we'd like to find the limit
Substitute the value, it won't take you a minute

If the value is undefined, and subbing just won't do
Rewrite the function, then it may come true

These are some techniques to help us on our way
Sometimes we need technology, to that, what can I say?

Limit Haiku

Something approaching
From both sides, called a limit
Calculus is cool

Derivatives and Tangent Lines

Finding the tangent to a curve at a point?
Sir Isaac newton derived to appoint

Points on the secant come closer and closer together
Tangent Line appearing, a derivative is better

Finding the slope of the tangent to the curve
Two points on the Secant Line converging, no swerve

F of X plus H, an infinitesimal number
Minus F of X, over H, to all newcomers

As H approaches the value of zero
You have a derivative, my true hero

Power Rule for Derivatives

Finding derivatives by the limit rule is cool
Until you learn the power rule

Just place the exponent out front of the term
Subtract one from it, we are here to learn

For the monomial term X to the N
We find the derivative down to the end

It's N times X to the power of N -1
This is how we have our fun

So listen to the lesson and have a good day
There is much more that I have to say

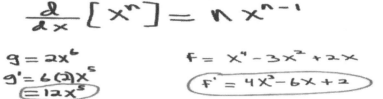

$$\frac{d}{dx}[x^n] = n\,x^{n-1}$$

$g = 2x^6$
$g' = 6(2)x^5$
$= 12x^5$

$f = x^4 - 3x^2 + 2x$
$f' = 4x^3 - 6x + 2$

Product rule

A thing about math class that's cool
We get to learn the product rule

Finding derivatives of functions multiplied
You'll be the star to those who have never tried

F prime G plus G prime F
There you have it, you'll pass the test

$$(fg)' = f'g + fg'$$

Quotient rule

When we want to divide two functions
The quotient rule for the derivative in conjunction

F prime G minus G prime F
Divide by G squared, I'll tell you the rest

Call it the quotient rule, it's learned in class
Unlock the secret, you'll be the big brass

Oh quotient rule you are so cool
You make it fun to learn in school

$$\left(\frac{f}{g}\right)' = \frac{f'g - g'f}{g^2}$$

Higher Order Derivatives

Higher order derivatives sound so complicated
Until you try them, no need to get frustrated

Just take the derivative again and again
It's how you do it, up to the end

The first and second derivatives are the main focus
You'll get through the course, with no hocus-pocus

So higher order derivatives are easy to calculate
They can get messy, I need to be straight

Chain Rule

Taking derivatives, learned in school
One must follow all the rules

When you have a function raised to a power
Use the chain rule, from that hour

Take the derivative of the outside part
Apply the power rule, from the very start

Multiply by the derivative of the inside function
You'll pass the next test, at least that's something

So pay careful attention to the examples I'm showing
Calculating derivatives will keep us going

Exponential Differentiation

It's the exponential function e to the x
The natural log's base, we differentiate next

A function whose derivative equals itself
Read it from a book upon my shelf

Sometimes you need to use the chain rule
Learn how to do this, you'll be really cool

Log Differentiation

A crowd favorite, log base e of X
It is only natural to differentiate next

Apply the chain rule taught in class
Take one over the argument, you'll learn real fast

It's the derivative of the function and the argument, too
Multiplied together, derivatives rule

So watch the lesson and examples
Differentiating logs, I'll give you some samples

Trigonometric Differentiation

Time to differentiate trigonometric functions
Sine and cosine are very good assumptions

The derivative of sine is simply cosine
Easy to remember, you'll do so fine

Differentiating cosine has got me reeling
You get the sine with a negative feeling

Don't forget and go off on a tangent
Secant squared its derivative imagined

The argument itself can be a function
Use the chain rule at this next junction

Pay careful attention to the examples I'll show
Winter break is near, I can't wait to go

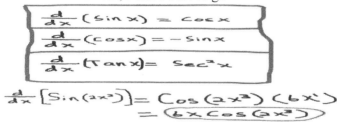

$$\frac{d}{dx}(\sin x) = \cos x$$
$$\frac{d}{dx}(\cos x) = -\sin x$$
$$\frac{d}{dx}(\tan x) = \sec^2 x$$

$$\frac{d}{dx}[\sin(2x^3)] = \cos(2x^3)(6x^2)$$
$$= 6x^2\cos(2x^3)$$

Extreme on an Interval

Maximums or minimums on a closed interval
Are called Extrema, don't forget you were told

On any closed interval, it can be seen
Continuous function takes all values between

At least one is an min and one is a max
Intuitively obvious, a natural fact

For max and mins not at endpoints
Tangent line is horizontal at that point

Derivative equals zero, where tangent's horizontal
Called a critical number, no need for orthodontal

One more thing, it's also true
Undefined values are critical, too

An extreme value theorem and a derivative test
I just can't wait to tell you the rest

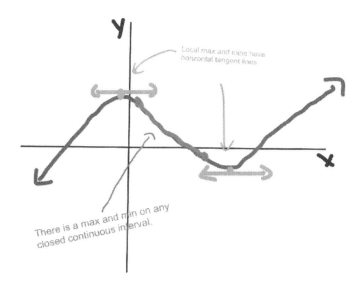

1st Derivative Test

A scary lesson, yes, indeed
A Derivatives test is what we need

Learning to find a max or a min
Of the function, from within

Take the first derivative and set to zero
Critical Numbers will make you a hero

Setup intervals using critical numbers
Find a test value in each one down under

Derivative changes positive to negative
You have a max, it's what you wanna give

You have a min when this is true
Negative to positive all the way through

So this is the first derivatives test
Watch the lesson, I'll explain the rest

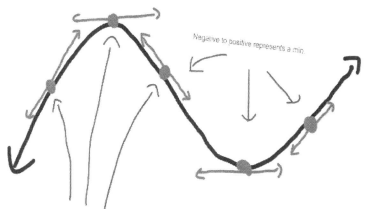

Negative to positive represents a min.

When the slope of the tangent line (derivative) goes from positive to negative, then the critical number is at the local max.

Second Derivative Test

A second test for derivatives
A polynomial function's narrative

Take the derivative of the function twice
Second derivatives will break the ice

Input the critical numbers too
Function's second derivative, nothing new

Second derivative a positive number
You have a minimum, why do you wonder?

Second derivative a negative
You have a max, that's how we live

Second derivative equal zero
Test fails, not our hero

This is the second derivative test
Do your homework and learn the rest

Let c be a critical number obtained by setting the
first derivative equal to zero or undefined, then if :

$$f''(c) > 0 \quad \text{Local min}$$

$$f''(c) < 0 \quad \text{Local max}$$

$$f''(c) = 0 \quad \text{test Fails}$$

Concavity

Time to test for concavity
No need for a dentist, as we'll see

Concave up or concave down
Second derivative gives you ground

Second derivative greater than zero
Concave up like Emperor Nero

Second derivative a negative number
Concave down and time to slumber

Second derivative zero or undefined
A point of inflection comes to mind

So pay attention to the lesson details
Make a smoothie and have some kale

Point of inflection. Where concavity switches over

Concave Down

Concave Up

Anti-Derivatives and Integrals

Today we learn to integrate
The antiderivative, so don't be late

Antiderivative, integral, synonymous
Derivative in reverse, so don't be anonymous

A derivative brings a function through
Antiderivative brings it back to you

It gives the area under the curve
Over the interval so I've heard

Listen to the lesson, I'll tell you more
I hope this poem was not a bore

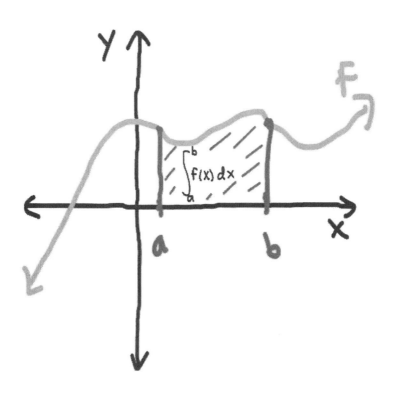

The Definite Integral

To find an area, it is without doubt
A definite integral carries good clout

Between the curve and the x-axis
Over an interval while doing our taxes

Truly definite, yes I'm sure
You find an area under the curve

Taking an integral from a to b
Clearly determined from what I see

Antiderivative at b minus a
The fundamental theorem will take you away

Listen to the lesson, let's be precise
Being definite, and surely concise

$$\int_2^7 x^2\,dx = \left.\frac{x^3}{3}\right|_2^7 = \frac{7^3}{3} - \frac{2^3}{3} = \frac{343}{3} - \frac{8}{3}$$

$$= \frac{335}{3} \text{ sq. units}$$

Integration by Substitution

Integrating the composition of F and G
Times G prime, what complexity

A U substitution will simplify
Your ability to integrate, so please don't cry

Just substitute a U for your G
Derivative du for G's primacy

Setting the integral with respect to U
Integrate normally, but you're not through

Substitute backwards to the original variable
Your antiderivative appears in stereo

Oh what power in U substitution
Integrals set free read the math constitution

Exponential Integration

An exponential function e to the x
Its own derivative read the text

Because of this we know it's true
Its antiderivative is e to the x to

For indefinite integrals look and see
Do not forget the constant C

It's all there is what I have to say
Let's do some examples and have a workday

Log Integration

The derivative of the natural log
It's one over X, let's clear the fog

So integrating the function one over X
Gives natural log, an antiderivatives best

Another very important skill
A U substitution is such a thrill

Find the antiderivative of one over U
Then back substitute, and then you're through

Please don't forget when the integral's indefinite
A constant C, now you're stepping it

Trig Integration

A thing about mathematics I love
Integrating trig functions, gentle like doves

Wise as serpents, I am telling thee
To integrate trig functions mathematically

Antiderivative of the sine,
Try to stay positive, it's negative cosine

To take an integral of cosine
A sine comes running, up from behind

You may just integrate secant squared
It equals tangent, so don't be scared

Once again for indefinite integrals
Remember the C, surely the way-to-go

Area Between Curves

Integrate the function, read the text
An area between the curve and the x

With two curves, one above the other
We find the area between, says my brother

Just subtract the upper from the lower
Next we integrate, like leaves in a blower

You find the area between two curves
Please drive safely, no need to swerve

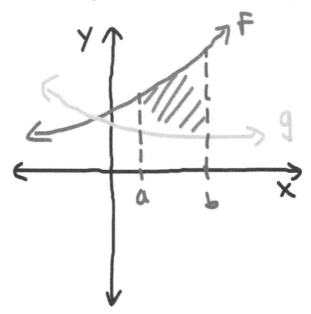

Area between f and g from a to b

$$\int_a^b f(x)dx - \int_a^b g(x)dx = \int_a^b (f-g)(x)\, dx$$

Disc Method for Volume

When you integrate across the interval
An area is found for tranquility visceral

Rotating area around the axis
Solid formed for volume clashes

Square the function, multiply by pi
Take the integral, I wonder why?

Volume obtained by infinite discs
Stacked together we'll take the risk

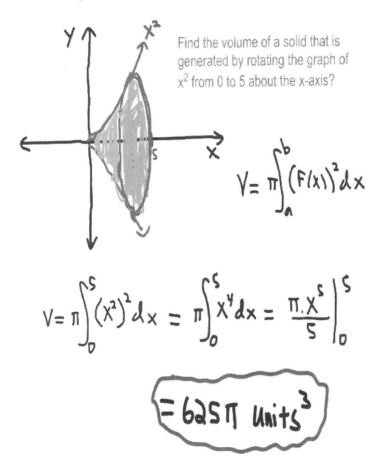

Find the volume of a solid that is generated by rotating the graph of x^2 from 0 to 5 about the x-axis?

$$V = \pi \int_a^b (F(x))^2 \, dx$$

$$V = \pi \int_0^5 (x^2)^2 \, dx = \pi \int_0^5 x^4 \, dx = \frac{\pi . X^5}{5} \Big|_0^5$$

$$= 625 \pi \text{ units}^3$$

Vectors

Now let's move to a brand new sector
We direct our study to that of vectors

A directed segment of a line
Its head and tail are just in time

Its length is called a magnitude
A quantity measured with attitude

It gives a velocity, time or force
Or just a direction to stay on course

Equal vectors, same magnitude and direction
Regardless of location, place or section

Combining vectors head to tail
A way to add them, the resultant sails

Divide a vector by its length
A unit vector has some strength

Next we have component form
Cartesian coordinates, a vector's born

Origin locates the vector's beginning
Head is the coordinate of the point, no kidding

To find the vector's magnitude
Coordinate form will get you through

Just sum the X and the Y value squared
Square root the result, please don't be scared

So many more examples yet to see
Watch the lesson, it'll set you free

Position Vectors

A vector drawn from a fixed position
From the origin, our next mission

Tail at origin, head to a point
Not a free vector, it's in the joint

Watch the lesson, your position is fixed
Staying put, right where you sit

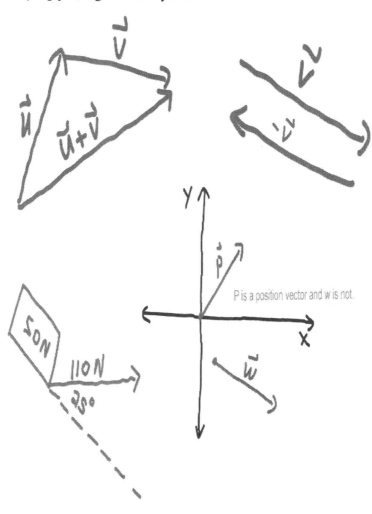

Scalar Product

Scalar, dot, or inner product
Mysterious terms, yet so parodic

They mean the same, yes it's true
Synonymous terms will get you through

Just match the vector's position components
Multiply together at that moment

Sum the result and then you're done
A scalar product will be won

$$\vec{u} = \begin{pmatrix} 2 \\ 3 \\ 4 \end{pmatrix} \quad \vec{v} = \begin{pmatrix} -1 \\ 4 \\ -2 \end{pmatrix} \quad \vec{u} \cdot \vec{v} = 2(-1)+3(4)+4(-2)$$

$$= -2 + 12 - 8 = \boxed{2}$$

$$|u| = \sqrt{2^2+3^2+4^2} \qquad |v| = \sqrt{(-1)^2+4^2+(-2)^2}$$

$$= \sqrt{29} \qquad\qquad = \sqrt{21}$$

$$\cos\theta = \frac{2}{\sqrt{29}\sqrt{21}}$$

Vector Equation of Line

Please don't step over it, a literary device
Very idiomatic, for vectors that's nice

For any two points, just one goes through
Vector equation of a line in cue

Sketch two vectors out to the points
Fixed at the origin, from the tail endpoint

Vector subtraction, to find the direction
Start from a point, no need for abjection

Analogous to slope and intercept form
The vector line, a mathematical norm

Sequences & Series

Set of numbers, put in order, according to a rule
Part of the next lesson you get to learn in school

We call the set a sequence, from one term to the next
A unique recurrence relation occurs throughout the text

When we sum them up, a series is thus formed
We use sigma notation, for this you've been forewarned

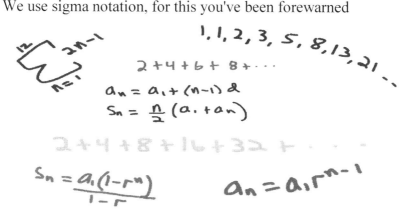

Arithmetic Sequences and Series

A common difference from term to term
Arithmetic sequence is our next concern

Recursive definition from previously
Next in sequence by adding d

Finding a term by its number
Nth term formula, no need to wonder

It's n minus one multiplied by d
Summed with the first, in the sequence, see

Next we find the series sum
Add them together and have some fun

Just combine the sequences first and last
Multiply by n over 2 and get the cash

Substituting nth term to the sum formula
Another way derived, to add them up for ya

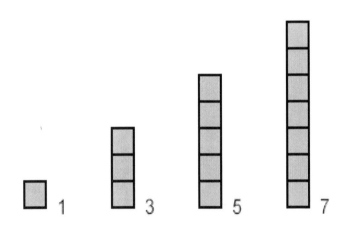

Geometric Sequences and Series

Studying the geometry of ratios and proportion
Geometric sequences come in for absorption

Each term multiplied by the ratio in common
We find the next one while snacking on ramen

R to the power of N minus 1
Times U1 is an nth term for fun

Next we find the series sum
A formula with exponents, please don't run

The difference of one and r to the n
Divided 1 minus r in the end

Multiply result by the sequence's first term
You find the sum without being burned

Do your homework and keep up in school
'Cause geometric sequences will make you no fool

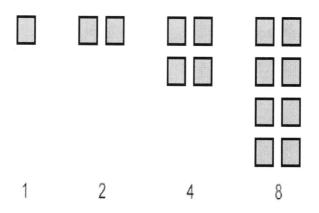

Measures of Central Tendency

Statistical measures, mean, median and mode
Are central measures from way back old

To find the mean just sum the numbers
Divide by how many in the set, no wonder

The median is the number in the middle
Just put them in order and play the fiddle

A favorite of mine is pi alamode
I have it most often so I call it my mode

These are just some of the measures of center
Statistical measures of the data to enter

Measures of Dispersion

This lesson comes without coercion
Statistical measures of the data's dispersion

We find the range from least to greatest
Max minus min you've heard the latest

The mean variation, squared from the mean
Called the variance, it's got to be seen

Square root of the variance for standard deviation
A measure of dispersion number one in the nation

Examples filled with frequencies and tables
Please pay attention as much as you are able

Cumulative Frequency

The total frequency tallied to the level
Numbers accumulate, no need to be disheveled

Median, quartiles, and interquartile range
Cumulative frequency tables sound so strange

Oh so useful for percentiles in data
From the table they pop out at ya

Measures of dispersion like interquartile range
75th percentile minus the 25th, so strange

Cumulative frequency tables are so cool
Just one of those things we love about our school

Box and Whiskers

The Min, Q1, median, Q3 and max
A five number summary, you need to just relax

Beautifully displayed on a box and whiskers plot
A five number summary really says a lot

The IQR is just the box's length
Range displayed from its whiskers are its strength

Oh box with whiskers, no need for a shave
Let's grow them out and live in a cave

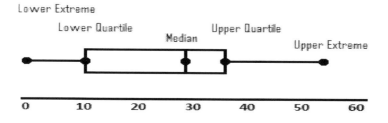

Histogram

Our next kind of graph is so historical
Grouped or continuous data allegorical

Frequency density is the height of the bar
Frequency divided by the width so far

Visual representation of the data's shape
A normal distribution will help you escape

Study and learn your histograms
On the next test, you won't need to scram

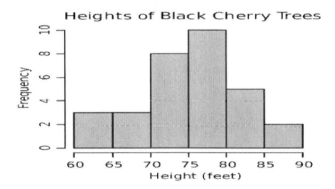

Random Variables

A variable that covers different outcomes
Range of possible, discreetly then some

Random variables in probability
Total possibilities as far as I see

Add the probabilities from the table
Sum is one when possibilities prevail

Expected value a weighted average
Outcomes times the probability savage

The Normal Distribution

Evenly distributed, a symmetrical shape
Very large sample of bananas gone ape

Shape of a bell or an antique clock
Normal distributions are new to the block

Mean is zero, standard deviation is one
Standard Normals are so much fun

Number of deviations above or below the mean
Called a Z score, they'll think you're so keen

Finding percentiles, probabilities reliable
Statistical methods so truly viable

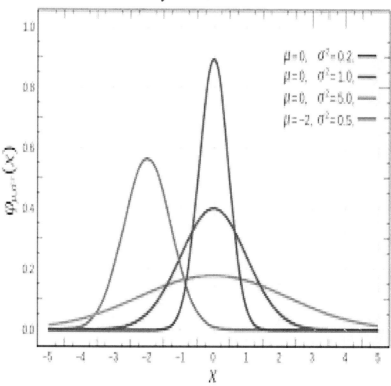

THANKS FOR READING MY BOOK
I APPRECIATE THE TIME IT TOOK

WHOEVER THOUGHT MATH AND POETRY
COULD BLEND TOGETHER SO NATURALLY?

MAYBE SOMEDAY
WHEN I'M PASSING YOUR WAY

WE COULD REFLECT MATHEMATICALLY
AND DO SOME POETRY

Made in the USA
Middletown, DE
20 December 2017